17 Anti-Procrastination Hacks: How to Stop Being Lazy, Overcome Procrastination, and Finally Get Stuff Done

By Dominic Mann

Table of Contents

Introduction

Victor Hugo was quite a man. He is one of the greatest and best-known writers France has ever produced. Among his many incredible works are such classics as *Les Misérables* and *The Hunchback of Notre Dame*.

His works and accomplishments are considered to be so great that his portrait was placed on the French banknotes.

From all this, you wouldn't be alone in assuming that this seemingly ultra-productive man of such immense accomplishment should be what all of us frustrated procrastinators aspire to be. That the great Victor Hugo was the epitome of motivated productivity and procrastination's antithesis.

Well, this assumption—surprisingly—couldn't be further from the truth. The great French poet and novelist suffered from terrible bouts of procrastination.

In late 1829, Hugo made an agreement with his publisher: He would write a new book titled, *"The Hunchback of Notre Dame*. Unfortunately, the famous French author managed to find more interesting things to do. Instead of writing the book, Hugo spent the next year—that's right, *year*—pursuing other projects, entertaining guests, and endlessly partying.

Understandably, his publisher had finally had enough of all the endless procrastination and so took matters into their own hands, deciding to issue him a deadline. And a formidable deadline it was. Due by February 1831, Hugo had less than six months to finish the book.

Despite the tight deadline, Hugo—the master procrastinator he was—still found himself not doing any work. So Hugo devised a clever plan to combat his unkillable urge to procrastinate: He would strip himself butt-naked and have his servant hide his clothes, not returning them until the appointed hour.

Unable to leave the house and go distract himself, Hugo remained in his study each day, writing furiously until he finally finished the book.

The strategy worked and *The Hunchback of Notre Dame* was published two weeks early.

And it's not just Victor Hugo,

Herman Melville used to have his wife literally chain him to his desk in order to get himself to finish the epic novel, *Moby Dick*. Unsurprisingly, this extreme method worked. Not only did he finish the book, but *Moby Dick* is now almost universally listed as one of the greatest works of fiction ever written.

Likewise, a bout of procrastination forced Frank Lloyd Wright—the great American architect—to design his most famous house in less than two hours. Yes, you read that right: Two hours.

In 1934, a wealthy Pittsburgh businessman named Edgar Kaufmann Sr., commissioned Wright to create a house in rural Pennsylvania—Fallingwater. In November, Wright went over and took a look at the site and wrote to assure Kaufmann that he was working on the plans. In reality, though, Wright hadn't so much as pulled out a piece of drawing paper.

Much to Wright's surprise (and likely horror), Kaufmann called him up early one Sunday morning in the September of 1935, announcing that he was on his way over and looking forward to seeing the design.

In the time it took Kaufmann to drive up from Pittsburgh, Wright calmly finished his breakfast and—with a group of extremely nervous apprentices watching on—drew up the plans for the house. Funnily enough, Fallingwater was listed as a National Historic Landmark in 1966, and is listed by the Smithsonian Institution as one of the 28 places "to visit before you die."

The problem of procrastination is not a new one, either.

Even thousands of years ago, men and women wrestled with the perils of procrastination. Demosthenes, an ancient

Greek orator, would shave one side of his head in order to force himself to stay indoors and practice speeches for fear of ridicule—not all that different a solution to Victor Hugo's hide-your-clothes method.

Despite procrastination having plagued humankind since the beginning of history, it *can* be defeated. And no, you don't need to hide your clothes or chain yourself to a desk.

Procrastination is, undoubtedly, a massive problem. It is the cause of immeasurable frustration. It can stop us from achieving our goals. It burdens us with stress, anxiety, and an unpleasant combination of self-loathing and guilt. Worst of all, procrastination prevents us from reaching our full potential.

Fortunately, procrastination is something that can be overcome—and that's exactly what this book is for. This book contains a carefully curated collection of techniques and approaches to overcoming procrastination and finally getting things done.

So dive right in and discover the most effective ways to beat procrastination and, in the process, achieve your goals.

1. Why Intelligent People Procrastinate (And How Not To)

Once upon a time, there lived an intellectually challenged gentleman. His finger would constantly be burned on stove tops and pricked by thorny rose bushes. The reason these undoubtedly painful event kept on happening again and again was because this poor man was unable to foresee the consequences of his actions. Whereas a Grandmaster of chess might see seven moves ahead, or an entrepreneur might be able to visualize their business strategy, the mental handicap of this fictional man allows no such ability.

This makes him fun at parties—after all, he's pretty much permanently drunk. He says and does things while mentally incapable of foreseeing the consequences.

Counterintuitively, though, this dullard is jaw-droppingly productive. No joke.

Procrastination? He's literally never done it. Never. Not once. He tackles tasks head on and gets them done lightning fast.

Now, how on earth is this?

Here's how: He is unable to foresee how difficult, tedious, and enjoyable doing the task will be. Consequently, all motivation and temptation to procrastinate is gone. He just does stuff without thinking about it.

Ironically, for this reason, intelligent people are more often the ones that feel the urge to procrastinate. This is because they are more likely to see and think about the consequences. It's going to be boring. It's going to be difficult. I might make a mistake. What if it's not done properly? I don't want to do this! And on. And on. And on again. Our intelligence ends up being used against us—to foresee how tedious and unpleasant doing a certain task will be, demotivating us in the process.

But the dummies of the world often just do whatever is in front of them. No thoughts of consequences. No thoughts of anything much, really. They just plow on like a mindless tractor.

But there's a lot that us procrastinators can learn from these inadvertently productive people. Us procrastinators, the smart people we are, often end up placing ourselves in a psychological jail-cell. As a result, we end up procrastinating! We discourage and demotivate ourselves, causing ourselves to procrastinate, by overthinking.

So what is it that we can learn from all this?

Well, first of all, our bodies have a visceral response to

the thoughts and images we feed it.

If we see someone accidentally slice their finger while chopping up fruits, we cringe and feel—at least in a certain way —as if we too had just cut our fingers.

The same thing happens when we start thinking about doing our taxes and any other not-so-enjoyable work that needs to get done. A mere glance at your tax form or to-do list can send intelligent brains on a mental tangent of negative thought-patterns that go so deep they paralyze one from taking action.

Unfortunately, all of this over-thinking not only gets us nowhere but it freezes us. This is best summed up by the following Chinese proverb: "Talk does not cook rice."

So what's the solution?

Develop the "next action" habit...

2. Develop the Next Action Habit

"The secret of getting ahead is getting started. The secret of getting started is breaking your complex overwhelming tasks into small manageable tasks, and starting on the first one."
— *Mark Twain*

In his book *Getting Things Done,* David Allen jokingly writes, "So what's the solution? There's always having a drink. Numb it. Dumb it down." He notes that alcohol suppresses people's negative self-talk and "uncomfortable visions," giving them an initial energy boost.

Taking the cue from the effects of alcohol, Allen discusses the power of "intelligently dumbing down your brain by figuring out the next action."

What does he mean by this?

Allen suggests shifting your focus from all the possible negative outcomes and unpleasantries—overwhelming and stressing you out in the process—to simply taking the next tiny physical action.

Open up keynote or PowerPoint and name your presentation. Or search Google for some images to put in your presentation. Or write the first five words of that article or blog post.

To stop procrastinating, shift your focus from the overwhelming immensity of the entire forest (i.e. project) to just a single tree (i.e. a small task). Focus only on the next physical action needed to move forward and do it.

The reason this is one of the most effective ways to combat procrastination is because you shift your focus from something overwhelming to something your mind perceives as doable. Rather than feeling overwhelmed (and thus tempted to procrastinate), your mind enthusiastically says, "Hey, I can do this! It's easy as!"

Although nothing changes in reality, this shift of focus makes a huge difference. It's the difference that makes a difference.

So whenever you feel the urge to procrastinate creeping its way back again, break down whatever you are doing into something smaller, simpler, more doable.

3. Build Momentum: The Physics of Productivity

"An object in motion tends to remain in motion along a straight line unless acted upon by an outside force."
— Isaac Newton

In 1686, Isaac Newton published his three laws of motion in *Principia Mathematica Philosophiae Naturalis*. In this publication he wrote his first law of motion as follows:

"Every body persists in its state of rest, or of uniform motion in a right line, unless it is compelled to change that state by forces impressed upon it."

Interestingly enough, Newton's first law of motion applies to more than just the movement of heavenly bodies.

You see, productive people tends to stay productive. Or, as they say, "Nothing succeeds like success."

Productive people tend to get one thing done, then another, and another. One thing spurs them on to the next, and the next. They build up momentum and that pushes them along.

Similarly, just as objects at rest remain at rest, unproductive people tend to remain unproductive. Procrastinators tend to continue to procrastinate—at least until they get a bit of momentum going for themselves, that is.

This is yet another reason that developing a "next action" habit is so effective. Getting started is often the hardest part, and once you get started, it's much easier to keep being productive.

One small step leads to another. And another. And yet another again. On and on and on. And before you know it, you've built up a wave of momentum and you are gliding through tasks like a Newtonian object glides through outer space.

This is also why many ultra-successful leaders and entrepreneurs develop powerful morning routines. By having a powerful start to their mornings, they create a wave of momentum that lasts all day—hurtling them through an ultra-productive day like an asteroid through space.

Focus on procrastinating and you'll find that momentum rolls in that direction.

Focus on taking action and you'll find that momentum rolls in that direction.

Speaking of taking action, there's one more thing you

need to remember...

4. Make a Tasty To-Do List

Most people make to-do lists that are, well, disgusting. Like brussel sprouts or fish-head soup.

They have things like "Taxes" or "Quarterly report". Yuck!

So how do you make your to-do list yummier?

First, realize that the things on your to-do-list either attract you or repel you. The way to make things yummier and more attractive is to make them *actionable*.

Instead of putting "New tires" on your to-do list, put "Call tire store for prices." Which one do you think you're more likely to procrastinate on? The former is unattractive, yucky, and not very actionable, while the latter is yummy-looking because it's very actionable.

Procrastination is best defeated by intelligently dumbing yourself down. Reduce your focus to no more than, "what is the very next physical action I can take? What is the *next action*?"— and then do it.

Make these little actions simple, easy, and actionable. They should be like tasty little nibbles. Repeat this simple process several times and you will find yourself gaining momentum, sending you hurtling through tasks like an asteroid.

5. The Two-Minute Rule

As we just discussed, one of the reasons people procrastinate is because they feel overwhelmed. Tasks seems too big. They look painful and unpleasant. And so we end up procrastinating. The best way to combat this, as we discussed, is to develop a next action habit and chunk tasks down into little tasty nibbles.

Unfortunately, we often also end up avoiding little tasks along the way—such as quickly answering a short email or doing the laundry—and these all add up, requiring us to put in a Herculean effort just to catch up.

Nobody wants to spend the weekend sorting through hundreds of unread emails and washing that mountain of clothes that's been piling up for the last month or so. As a result, we just end up procrastinating even more.

That's where the two-minutes rule comes in. If something takes less than two minutes to do, do it now. Just get it out of the way. No more drowning in your inbox or having your apartment look like a landfill. If something takes less than two minutes, take care of it immediately.

The two-minute rule also applies to habits. If you're building a new habit, make sure it takes no longer than two minutes to execute. Otherwise, you're unlikely to consistently execute that habit long enough for it to become automatic.

Apply the the two-minute rule to your life and you'll find that you're always on top of things. Tasks will no longer pile up into massive mountains of work that are just begging to be procrastinated on.

The same goes for habits. If you want to make a habit of eating healthier, just grab a piece of fruit and eat it—it'll take less than two minutes. And do it the next day, and the next. Furthermore, because of Newton's productivity-applicable law of motion (objects in motion remain in motion, and vice versa), you'll likely find yourself starting to make salads, choosing water over soda, bananas over donuts, and so on. Likewise, if you want to make a habit of reading, just read the first page of a new book—it'll take less than two minutes. Once again, thanks to Newton's first law, you'll probably zoom through three chapters without even realizing it. Similarly, if you want to make a habit of exercising, just chuck on some running shoes and go out the front door—it'll take less than two minutes. And, once again thanks to Newton's first law, you'll probably end up going for a 20-minute run plus 30 push ups when you get back.

Procrastination is almost always solved by simply taking the first step. The biggest obstacle to productivity is just getting started. Once you do that, everything else tends to fall into place.

So just get started. As Lao Tzu said "A journey of thousand miles must begin with a single step." Just write the first five words of that article or press release. Just eat one apple. Floss one tooth. Do a single push up. Everything else will fall into place. That's the power of the two-minute rule. Once you get started—no matter how small or insignificant the action may seem—the ball starts rolling. One thing leads to another. Momentum builds. And before you know it, procrastination has long since disappeared from the rear-view mirror. But when it does creep back upon you once again, just pull out the two-minute rule, restart the engine, and all will be right. But don't worry about any of that. Just take one step. That first step. That's all that matters.

6. Set Macro Goals and Micro Quotas

Anthony Trollope was one of the most successful writers of the 19th century. He wrote 47 hugely popular novels, along with 18 non-fiction books, and numerous short stories, plays, and articles.

The most surprising thing about Trollope, though, is that he achieved all this despite working a 9-5 job at the post office, doing his writing between 5:30am and 8:30am each morning.

Now, writing a full-sized novel is no small feat. In fact, it is far from uncommon for would-be novelists to quickly find themselves overwhelmed and, as a result, either quit or procrastinate themselves into oblivion. I'm sure you can, unfortunately, emphasize with this.

So what was it that made Anthony Trollope different? How did he avoid the all-too-common pitfall of feeling overwhelmed and procrastinating?

Well, Trollope developed a strategy that can be summed up as follows: Set macro goals and micro quotas.

Obviously, Trollope's macro goals consisted of writing full-length novels. So what were his micro-quotas? (Keep in mind that "micro quotas" are basically little goals—or "quotas"—that moves one towards the achievement of their "macro goal").

Well, here's Trollope's secret: Each morning after rising at 5:00am, he would be seated at his desk by 5:30am and employ the following anti-procrastination strategy, which he describes in his book, *Autobiography*:

"It had at this time become my custom,—and is still my custom, though of late I have become a little lenient of myself—to write with my watch before me, and to require of myself 250 words every quarter of an hour.

"This division of time allowed me to produce over ten pages of an ordinary novel volume a day, and if kept through ten months, would have given as its results three novels of three volumes each in the year..."

At first glance, Trollope's approach seems dead simple. Despite the simple appearance of Trollope's approach, it is ridiculously effective, and for so many reasons. Let's take a look at just some of those reasons and see what we can learn.

First of all—and most importantly—big projects, regardless of whether they take months to complete, or days, or in some cases, even hours, can be overwhelming and frustrating due to the sheer volume of work and time required. That said, it's not so much the immensity of the work required nor the overwhelming length of time needed for its completion that's the problem. The true problem lies in the fact that we lose any sense of accomplishment or satisfaction at having completed something. It feels like we're swimming across the Pacific Ocean with no end in sight. As a result, we procrastinate. And procrastinated. And thanks again to Newton's first law, we continue to procrastinate forever.

So what's the solution? And what can we learn from Anthony Trollope who, in writing full-length novel after full-length novel, pretty much swam across the Pacific not once, but several dozen times.

Well, Trollope divided up the immense work of writing a novel—we'll continue the analogy of swimming across the Pacific—into laps up and down a 25 meter (82 feet) swimming pool.

Now, why is this so effective?

Well, I'm sure you can relate to how frustrating and disheartening it can be to be stuck doing a single task for an extending period of time. It feels like it's taking forever, there's no sense of accomplishment or satisfaction. It begins to get discouraging. And so on.

Trollope's solution overcomes this by finding a different source from which to drive that feeling of encouraging and motivating feeling. Books can take months (or years) to complete. That wasn't going to work. Even chapters can take several days. That wouldn't work either. So Trollope's solution was to measure his progress in 15-minutes increments.

With this approach, Trollope gets a regular dosage of motivating feelings of accomplishment. He doesn't need to wait months for the book nor days for whole chapters. He gets these small wins every 15 minutes.

Even if you are not a novelist like Trollope, there is much you can learn from this approach.

First of all, small indicators of progress spur you to do more and more. You gain momentum and become significantly more likely to finish the task.

Secondly, these little accomplishments—much like an effective morning routine—help to quickly develop your day into one with an attitude of effectiveness and productivity.

One of the most common reasons we procrastinate is because we feel intimidated and overwhelmed. But this doesn't mean you should stop dreaming big or taking on challenging tasks and projects in order to avoid the temptation to procrastinate. By far the most effective approach is to follow Trollope's lead. Find a way to balance the satisfaction of getting things done and pursuing your biggest and most ambitious goals by setting "macro goals" and "micro quotas".

As Anthony Trollope himself said, "I found it to be expedient to bind myself by certain self-imposed laws"—for, as Trollope also said, "A small daily task, if it be really daily, will beat the labours of a spasmodic Hercules."

You get the best of both worlds: The motivation of pursuing an inspiring long-term goal as well as the motivation derived from small accomplishments and seeing your progress along the way. When it comes to big projects and long-term goals, there's no better way to beat the temptation to procrastinate.

7. Time Blocks

One of the keys to overcoming procrastination is learning to become committed to getting stuff done. Not committed as in, "Yeah, I'd like to get that done." Rather, committed as in, "I'm going to do this at X time on X day at X location."

In fact, studies have found that committing to an activity in this way is indeed one of the most effective ways at overcoming procrastination. While only a small minority people who say they want to do an activity—in the case of this particular study, exercising—actually do it, almost everybody who was told to schedule an exact location, time, and type of exercise did it. And such is the power of using time blocks to overcome procrastination.

Without truly committing to doing an activity—such as by specifying exactly when, where, and how you will do a specific task—procrastination just becomes too easy. So let's take a look at several ways to use this incredibly powerful anti-procrastination technique.

First of all, and perhaps most obviously, you need to decide exactly what it is you need to get done. Though simple, simply knowing exactly what you need to get done is surprisingly powerful.

During this time block, eliminate everything else. Put your devices on airplane mode, take advantage of website blocking tools, etc. Seriously. Today's increasingly powerful multipurpose devices—such as tablets, laptops, computers, and phones—succumbing to the urge to procrastinate is far too easy. Millions of interesting (yet unproductive) sites are literally a click away. As soon something starts to get a little boring or difficult, procrastinating ends up easier than just soldiering on. So make it so it's easier to just continue working (such as by using website blocking tools). We tend to follow the path of least resistance, so use this fact to your advantage.

Another way to get around this is to do tasks that require internet usage ahead, and then turn it off, buckle down, and dive into a session (i.e. time block) of undistracted work with no chance of—or option for—procrastination. This is an especially great approach if you're doing a task that requires research such as a blog or article. Too often, it's too easy to fall into the trap of "researching" more than you really need to, or just "researching" unrelated topics.

That said, if you truly need the web, tools that I have personally found useful include *Go Fucking Work*, a timed website blocker for those of you that don't mind a bit of profanity, and *RescueTime*, an extension which keeps track of the time you spend of different websites and programs, providing you with an honest look at how you spend your time. Furthermore, you can—if you want—use these two programs in conjunction, putting temporary blocks (using *Go Fucking Work*) on websites you realize (using *RescueTime*) you're spending too much time on.

The point here is this: To truly overcome procrastination and get stuff done, you need to really, really commit. Set aside a block of time, cut out all distractions. And give yourself no choice but to do whatever it is you need to do.

8. The Butt-in-Chair Method

Amongst writers—especially novelists—this method of scheduling time blocks is known as the "butt-in-chair" method. This 100 percent effective anti-procrastination strategy, as the name implies, involves putting your butt in the chair at your desk for a certain period of time each day. No distractions. Nothing. Just you and your pen and paper (or word document). The butt-in-chair method doesn't require writing. You could just sit there and do nothing—as long as there are no distractions. Eventually, though, you just start writing. And almost every single time, at the end of the two hour (or however long) session, several pages of work will have materialized.

Even if your particular line of work isn't always compatible with the butt-in-chair anti-procrastination strategy, there is much we can learn from it.

The power of committing a block of undistracted time to working on a specific task cannot be overstated. Committing to an undistracted time block is perhaps the single most effective anti-procrastination technique there is.

Let's take a quick look at another variation of the butt-in-chair method that's become quite popular among entrepreneurs and executives...

9. Airplane Days

A surprising array of people has noted that they are at their most productive when they are 30,000 feet in the air.

Why is this? Is there something special about traversing the skies in an elongated aluminium tube that allows people to have some of their most productive work sessions?

Nope. It simply comes down to this: There are no distractions.

Nobody is popping in to say "Hi". There's no internet. No phone calls. No text messages. No emails. Nothing but them and their work. Flying inadvertently forces upon you the "butt-in-chair" strategy. And one of the consequences of the forceful extraction of distraction from a situation is that a massive amount of work gets done.

Fortunately, you don't need to dish out thousands of dollars and go on an international flight every time you need an ultra-productive work session. Instead, just pretend that you are going on an all-day flight. Get out of the office, block out of the day on your shared calendar if you have one, and put (and *keep*) all your devices on airplane mode. Today you are on an (imaginary) international flight. (Note that your boss might not be a big fan of this if you don't work for a more progressive company—but it's still worth a try.)

10. Create a Distraction To-Do List

A common problem I have personally encountered with procrastination is that I suddenly think of something—"I wonder what minimalist offices looks like" or "I wonder if Donald Trump has said another crazy thing that's blowing up on all the news sites"—and before you know it, 30 minutes have passed and I haven't got a damn thing done. (On a side note, studies have found that once we distract ourselves, it takes an average of 25 minutes to return to our original tasks—and on top of that, it takes about the same time to regain the intensity of focus we had before we distracted ourselves).

Thankfully, there's a solution. And it's not one of those solutions that hinge on willpower alone. You get to check out whatever interesting thing it was that you thought of and get your work done.

How is this possible?

Here's how: Create a "distraction to-do list".

Rather than succumbing to the temptation in the moment, simply write down whatever it is you want to do or thought of onto your "distraction to-do list" and get straight back to work. Later on, once all your important tasks are done, you will return to your "distraction to-do list" and freely indulge in it—without the guilt, and without sacrificing productivity.

11. The "(10+2)x5" Method

If you're a hardcore procrastinator and aren't sure you are quite ready for a full-on "airplane day" or lengthy undistracted time block, this anti-procrastination strategy will be perfect for you.

The brainchild of Merlin Mann at "43 Folders" (www.43folders.com), the "(10+2)x5"method requires no more than a timer and your to-do list.

So how's it work?

You sit down, set the timer for 10 minutes, and work with single-minded focus until the timer rings. For this 10 minutes do *only* work. Like, seriously. It's 10 minutes. Just hang in there, okay? No quick "research", nothing but working towards the completion of the task(s).

After your ten minutes of intense labor are up (phew), you get two minutes—no more, no less—to do whatever on earth you want. Coffee, Reddit, Facebook—anything. (Although I would strongly suggest you get up and walk around to let your mind refresh, it's ultimately up to you.)

After the two minutes are up, buckle down for another ten minutes of work and repeat the process.

So now you know what the "(10+2)" is for—but what about the "x5"?

This work-play cycle is to be repeated five times, giving you a total of 60 minutes (i.e. one hour) of working and breaking.

The point of this chaotic schedule is to make procrastination less tempting. After all, it's only ten minutes of work at time. Pretty dang easy. Furthermore, the chaotic nature of the schedule makes you end up looking forward to *both* the breaking and working—a nice change for once, eh?

Eventually, you'll end up skipping breaks and just working, and that's great! Often, the biggest hurdle to overcoming procrastination is simply getting started, getting into the flow, and building a little momentum. The "(10+2)x5" method is great for this as you only need to work in very short bursts and you gets lots of breaks, so it's easy to start. And once you do get warmed up, you're free to just fully dive into getting things done.

12. Utilize the Power of Deadlines

Somehow, college students are able to do an entire semester's work in a single (Red Bull fueled) night. No jokes. But how on earth do they do it? What's their secret to resisting any form of procrastinating and simply buckling down for immense sessions of work?

Here's the secret: Deadlines. There's simply no other way out. But once we're out of the education system, we often no longer encounter situations that are as black and white. Moreover, we don't have the ability to set deadlines that create that sort of pressure for ourselves.

Or do we?

Well, we actually can. Using services such as "stickK" (www.stickk.com) or by simply doing it ourselves, we can create precise deadlines that have tangible consequences if missed.

"stickK" is one such service that allows you to but money on the line, forcing you to either get your stuff done or lose out on cold hard cash. You even have the option of donating it to a charity you absolutely despise, adding moral pain to the financial pain. You might, for example, donate to the George W. Bush presidential library or Westboro Baptist Church.

13. Kill Your Inner Perfectionist

"The first draft of anything is shit."
— *Ernest Hemingway*

Science has shown us that the number one cause of procrastination is what they call "analysis paralysis." In layman's terms, "analysis paralysis" means being a perfectionist.

In fact, a study, "Perfectionism dimension and research productivity in Psychology Professors: Implications for understanding the (mal)adaptiveness of perfectionism, " published in the October 2010 issue of the Canadian Journal of Behavioral Science, found that perfectionist psychology professors are significantly less productive than their not-so-perfectionist peers. Surprise, surprise, right?

But wait, more shocking is the fact that these perfectionist professors produce fewer publications, garner less citation, and are far less likely to have their work published in high-impact journals. So not only are they less productive, their perfectionism is for naught.

In other words, these perfectionist psychology professors —counterintuitively—end up *hurting* their career as a result of their perfectionism.

Stephen King wrote in *On Writing*, "You can approach the act of writing with nervousness, excitement, hopefulness, or even despair—the sense that you can never completely put on the page what's in your mind and heart." (Note that this can apply to whatever your field of work is, whether it be design, sales, etc.)

You might hate to hear it, but nothing is perfect. Rather, everything is in the state of continuous evolution. We constantly learn, gain experience, and improve—but we're never perfect. When it comes to productivity, something is always better than nothing. Or, as the big red posters plastered around the Facebook offices say, "Done is better than perfect."

Leonardo da Vinci's "Mona Lisa"—the most famous painting on earth—is unfinished. That's right. You didn't read that wrong. Leonardo's contemporary, Giorgio Vasari, said that "after he had lingered over it for four years, [he] left it unfinished." Moreover, Leonardo himself said later in life that he regretted "never having completed a single work."

Seems crazy doesn't it? When it comes to perfectionists, Leonardo da Vinci is pretty hard to beat. Fortunately, Leonardo realized that something was better than nothing and did his work anyway, despite personally believing them to be imperfect and unfinished.

Whether you are a writer, architect, 9-5er, or psychology professor, you must learn to quit being a perfectionist. That doesn't mean doing crappy work. It just means learning when to stop. At a certain point, the law of diminishing returns kicks in and it becomes far more productive for you to move onto the next task.

As Jodi Picoult said, "You can't edit a blank page."

Likewise, David Ogilvy, arguably the best copywriter to have ever lived, said, "I am a lousy copywriter, but I am a good editor."

Xerox Killed by Perfectionism

Now, let's take a look at an example of failure due to perfectionism.

In 1973, Xerox made a mistake that caused them to miss out on the personal computing revolution and instead be annihilated by less perfectionist companies like Apple and Microsoft.

Why? Because other companies got stuff done and offered it to consumers. Their products might not have been perfect in every way (after all, nothing is), but they were good enough and, most importantly, available to consumers.

Unfortunately for Xerox, this wasn't the case. They had created a revolutionary new computer called the "Alto". It had a mouse. A graphical screen (as opposed to green lines of code) like we are familiar with today. It could display images and had the most intuitive graphical user interface that anyone had ever seen.

So why, then, did Xerox fail to become the leader in the personal computing industry? How did they let hundreds of billions of dollars slip through their fingers?

Here's why: Perfectionism.

They wanted to make it absolutely perfect. They wanted to combine it with their other breakthrough technologies, such as the laser printer and the Ethernet.

Because of their perfectionism, they needed everything to be "just right" the first time around. They wanted to completely reinvent the modern office.

So rather than releasing the "Alto" in 1973, they ended up releasing it—combined with all their other technologies—in 1981, renaming it the "Star". It was launched with much fanfare.

Xerox's perfect, completely reimagined modern office, the "Star", came at a $50,000 installation price.

Unfortunately for Xerox, that same year—1981—IBM introduced its PC (i.e. personal computer) for $1,565. Clearly more affordable.

IBM's PC was far from perfect and was significantly less impressive than Xerox's "Star", but it quickly became a hit product. It wasn't perfect, but it was affordable and it worked—and that was the most important thing.

A few years later, Microsoft came out with Windows and Apple came out with the Macintosh. Both of these, as we know, became runaway success.

Xerox could have released products that were just as good an entire decade before, but they let their perfectionism get in the way. They learned the hard way that something is always better than nothing.

Apparently learning from Xerox's mistake, Google's Gmail was in "beta" from its launch in 2005 until 2009—five years. By the time it left "beta", it was already the most popular email service on earth. That's pretty damn good for something that wasn't even considered finished. Imagine if Google had succumbed to the perfectionist urge to not release it until 2009. Gmail would not be nearly as successful as it is today.

Likewise, Ed Catmull, the founder of Pixar, says that "early on, all our movies suck." Catmull sees his job not as getting things perfect but helping get things from "suck to not-suck."

Most of the time, the solution is to just hit the ground running. No analysis paralysis or desire to make things 100 percent perfect the first time around. In fact, you would often be surprised at how well the human brain can do things when you just jump right into a situation—whether or not you're "prepared."

Force yourself to start a conversation with an attractive

stranger on the street and your brain will very quickly come up with things to say.

Accidentally fall into a lake with all your clothes on and, though you might not get an Olympic gold medal, you'll quickly find yourself swimming just fine.

Start writing some random stuff on a page and, soon enough, you'll get into the flow of things and that article, blog post, or novel will start taking shape.

So stop focusing on doing things *perfectly* and instead simply focus on *doing things*, period. Jump in headfirst, ready or not, and before you know it, you'll be swimming.

If your inner perfectionist is causing you to procrastinate, just keep this in mind: You can't edit a blank page.

14. How to Procrastinate Productively

Sometimes, we simply can't help but procrastinate—no matter how much we don't want to. We might be tired, mentally exhausted, or whatever. Sometimes it just happens, and we can't deny that.

The solution in this case is less obvious: Do things that are easier, but still productive. This is known as the redirect technique.

Rather than simply giving up for the day and plopping yourself in the couch in front of the television with a box of pizza, learn to utilize the redirect technique. Put simply, procrastinate productively.

Do some small task that still needs to get done, like returning some calls, replying to some emails, doing some simple planning or research, or finishing up some edits on an article. Then return to more productive tasks once you feel you're ready.

15. The Kind of Visualization That Leads to Procrastination (and the Kind That Leads to Action)

Many of us visualize success (or failure, or both!)—even if we don't realize it or believe in the practice. Unfortunately, many of us visualize success in a way that can actually lead to procrastination rather than help us to work toward our goals.

Why is this? Isn't visualization supposed to be good? Isn't that what all the self-described self-help guru's preach?

Well, consider the following. What would you do if you achieved your goal?

Most likely, you'd feel relieved, right? Finally, you can have a little bit of a break. Time to relax a little. You're a success!

Unfortunately, the same thing happens when we visualize success. Instead of being motivated to go out and make what we just pictured in our mind a reality, we trick our subconscious brain into believing we have actually already achieved our goals.

In fact, several studies have found that our bodies physically relax. We end up *less* likely to feel motivated to do what we need to do. More damning, we are actually *significantly* less likely to achieve that which we visualize. Ouch!

Researchers Gabriele Oettingen and Heather Oettingen published a paper in the "Journal of Experimental Social Psychology" suggesting that not only is positive visualization ineffective, but that it is counterproductive.

They found that positive visualization of success resulted in the draining of energy and ambition. Heart rate decreases, blood pressure lowers, and our brain is tricked into thinking that all is well in the fantasy land of success in our mind. Time to kick back and relax!

In one study, the researchers showed that thirsty, water-deprived participants experienced an energy drain as a result of visualizing a glass of icy cold water.

They also found that participants who were told to visualize succeeding at their goals throughout the week ended up achieving significantly fewer goals than those told to think about the challenges they faced in any way they liked. Even more interesting is that the positive visualizers actually reported feeling less energetic than the other group—and physiological tests backed up these lethargic sentiments.

So what's the solution, then?

Firstly—and most obviously—stop excessively visualizing success. Instead of visualizing the outcome, visualize the *process* of achieving that desirable outcome. For example, rather than visualizing getting a good job, visualize applying for lots and lots of jobs, going through job interviews, and taking all the necessary steps to achieving your goals. *Visualize the process, not the outcome.* (As a side note, one study found that people who visualized getting a good job applied for less jobs and ended up getting a job at a lower salary than their non-visualizing counterparts.)

Likewise, rather than visualizing getting top marks, visualize doing all the necessary study needed to consistently get good grades.

Take the approach of world-class athletes and Olympians when it comes to visualization. They don't visualize standing on the highest spot on the podium triumphantly holding aloft their gold medal. What they do instead is visualize the race. The start, the motion of their body, the course (if applicable), pushing the boundaries of their pain threshold, overcoming any unexpected obstacles they may face during the event, and so on. They visualize the *process* of winning gold (or setting a world record), not the *outcome*.

16. The One Word That Kills Procrastination

Another factor that can cause procrastination is the way we view ourselves—our self-image.

Researchers at the University of Houston and Boston College found that our self-talk can have a huge impact on our behavior and whether or not we do something.

This effect is so pronounced, in fact, that the researchers discovered that something as simple as swapping the word "can't" with "don't" can have a huge impact on our actions. It can make the difference between whether we take a good action—say, declining that chocolate cake or going to the gym— or taking a not-so-good action—say, eating that slice of chocolate cake or skipping the gym yet again.

While the words "can't" and "don't" may seem largely interchangeable, they actually have a difference in psychological impact.

Telling yourself (or others) that you "can't" do something impresses upon the mind that you would very much like to do the thing in question but you're denying yourself of it. That you're exerting willpower, such as if someone tells themselves (or others) that "I can't skip gym".

The word "don't", on the other hand, is far more empowering. Imagine somebody saying "I don't drink alcohol" or "I don't eat unhealthy foods" or "I don't skip gym." By using the word "don't", you impress upon the mind the idea that you're not the kind of person who skips gym or eats junk food.

Still not convinced?

At the end of the study, the researchers offered participants the choice of either a granola bar or chocolate bar as a token of appreciation for their involvement. The participants who had been taught to say "I don't" were almost twice as likely (64 percent versus 39 percent) to choose the healthier option than the "I can't" participants.

Likewise, it was found that participant working towards a goal related to health and fitness were *eight* times more likely to take a bad action (such as skip the gym or eat some junk food) if they told themselves "I can't". While eight out of ten of those using the "I don't" strategy were able to resist such temptations, that figure dropped to a staggering one out of ten when it came to those using the "I can't" strategy.

So if ever you catch yourself telling yourself (or others) that you *can't* have this or do that, simply swap it for a "I *don't* do this."

17. How to Cheaply and Quickly Outsource Tasks

Now, outsourcing might not seem like much of a solution to procrastination. And that's because it's not. You're basically continuing to procrastinate, and just getting the work done by shrugging it off to somebody else.

While this isn't necessarily the best way to resolve procrastination, outsourcing is nonetheless worth some consideration.

Although not always the case, sometimes even the very best of us can succumb to the irresistible urge to procrastinate when it comes to tasks that are boring, tedious, draining, and repetitive. Although this book focuses on overcoming procrastination, here's a little productivity tip: These are not the kind of tasks you want to spend your willpower and mental energies on. It is better to focus on more important and productive activities. So often the best solution is to simply outsource them.

The way to go about outsourcing can vary depending on the task, however two great options to get started are *Upwork* (https://upwork.com/) and *Fiverr* (https://fiverr.com/).

Upwork is a platform on which you can post specific jobs and search millions of freelancers of all different skills. You can also find extraordinarily cheap assistants that you can hire to help out with certain tasks or aspects of your work for anywhere from US$3 to US$5 an hour.

Fiverr is different to *Upwork* in that you search pre-existing "gigs" that people have put up, and you pay $5 for a specific task to be done. Gigs range from editing a specific number of words, to recording a voiceover, to doing graphic design, to doing social media promotion.

If you're burdened by tasks that are not only easy to procrastinate on but are also huge time sucks and not all that productive, it might be worth considering outsourcing them. Spend your time on engaging, high value tasks.

Summary and Conclusion

"You may delay, but time will not."
— *Benjamin Franklin*

"The best way to get something done is to begin."
— *Unknown*

"Begin to weave and God will give you the thread."
— *German Proverb*

I could write a big, fancy conclusion, but that will not help you.

I could try to motivate you into taking action, but—in the long term, at least—that will not help you.

Instead, here is a quick recap of the 17 strategies discussed in this book.

***

Anti-Procrastination Hack #1: Make yourself a little dumber. Stop overthinking everything. Stop visualizing in your mind's eye the unpleasantness and joylessness of whatever it is you need to do. Just plow on like a dummy.

Anti-Procrastination Hack #2: Think only in terms of the very next physical action you need to take. Rather than overwhelming yourself with massive, seemingly impossible tasks, think only of the "next action." For example, that might be writing an opening sentence, starting up PowerPoint and giving it a title, or calling the car repair shop for tire prices.

Anti-Procrastination Hack #3: Use the power of small wins to build momentum. As they say, "nothing succeeds like success." Once you start being productive, it becomes exponentially easier to continue being productive. The most important thing is to just get started.

Anti-Procrastination Hack #4: Make your to-do list a tasty one. How do you make your to-do list yummy? By making it *actionable*. Rather than just plopping a bunch of tasks on it, write down the *actions* you need to take.

Anti-Procrastination Hack #5: Use the two-minute rule to prevent overload. If a task takes less than two minutes, do it right away. If you procrastinate on all these tasks long enough—which at first seem tiny and insignificant—they'll quickly build up and you'll find yourself overwhelmed.

Anti-Procrastination Hack #6. Break big, overwhelming goals down into bite-sized nibbles. It's good to dream big, but big things are also easy to procrastinate on. Fix this by creating small "sub-goals" which move you toward the completion of your larger goal.

Anti-Procrastination Hack #7: Write down exactly when, where, and what you are going to do. Studies show that by writing down the specifics of what you need to do as well as *when* and *where* you will do it, you make it almost certain that the task will actually get done.

Anti-Procrastination Hack #8: Stick your butt in a chair and don't leave for an hour. Or two hours. Or half an hour. Whatever works for you. No distractions. No Facebook or Reddit. None of that. You *can* just sit there and do nothing. But you'll quickly find yourself just starting to work anyway. This is also known as the "butt-in-chair" method.

Anti-Procrastination Hack #9: Pretend you're catching an airplane. Put all your devices on airplane mode for a set period of time, go find a quiet place to work, and get going. Once your airplane "lands", you can turn off airplane mode on all your devices. I recommend having an "airplane day" at least once a week for a serious productivity boost.

Anti-Procrastination Hack #10: Make a "to-do" list for your distractions. Are you diligently working when all of a sudden an idea pops in your head? "I just had a thought, let's go Google what a standing desk looks like," or "What is the origin of the phrase, 'crossing the Rubicon'? Let's search it up on Wikipedia." No. Pull out a piece of paper and write all these distractions/things you want to do, then go right back to work. Once you've finished working, you can go through your "distraction to-do list" guilt-free.

Anti-Procrastination Hack #11: Try the "(10+2)x5 Method." In other words, work for 10 minutes (yes, seriously, it's only 10 minutes—just do it!) and then break/procrastinate for two minutes. Repeat this five times for a total of one hour of working and breaking. After about an hour of doing this, you'll find yourself sick of the constant breaking and wanting to just continue working (what a nice change, for once!). Ta da!

Anti-Procrastination Hack #12: Set yourself a deadline. A serious deadline. If you don't meet this deadline, donate a predetermined sum of money to a charity you absolutely despise. If you can't trust yourself to do that, get an accountability buddy or use a service such as https://www.stickk.com/.

Anti-Procrastination Hack #13: Make "done is better than perfect" your new motto. Seriously. One is more than zero, even if you were aiming for 10. You can't edit a blank page, so kill your inner perfectionist and just do it anyway—even if it's not worthy of a Nobel prize.

Anti-Procrastination Hack #14: Start procrastinating productively when you no longer feel like working. Mentally fatigued and feel like you can't do anymore? Well, before you open up Facebook, start doing some less mentally demanding (but still productive) tasks such as responding to some emails, making a call, finding pictures for your PowerPoint presentation, lightly editing an article, and so on.

Anti-Procrastination Hack #15: Visualize the *process* not the outcome. Don't visualize hopping on your private jet to fly to Monaco for a holiday on your new 230 ft superyacht. Rather, visualize the *process*—the work and things you need to do—of achieving that level of success (i.e. the outcome).

Anti-Procrastination Hack #16: Never tell yourself you "can't" do something. Rather, tell yourself that you *"don't"* do it. Saying, "I don't eat unhealthy food" is far more empowering than saying, "I can't eat unhealthy food." And it shows. Using the word "don't" (both to others and in your own self-talk) has been scientifically shown to double the likelihood that you'll choose the better/healthier option.

Anti-Procrastination Hack #17: Outsource mundane tasks instead of procrastinating on them. If you're procrastinating on a bunch of boring, mundane, menial tasks, consider simply outsourcing them (or delegate).

***

Whenever you find yourself struggling to get yourself to do something, review these summary points and get on your way.

The fact that you've read this book to the very end proves that you *do* in fact have what it takes to overcome procrastination. Now all you need to do is put this book down and get going!

Good luck!

Made in the USA
Middletown, DE
29 March 2018